The Great Girls Network Series

Confessions of a Recovering Helpaholic

By Margery Miller, founder, Great Girls Network

Confessions of a Recovering Helpaholic

Published by PeopleBiz Inc.
214 Murray Lane
Richardson, TX 75080

ISBN: 978-1-7329373-0-7

Cover design by Ariana Levya
Illustrations by Lida Keene
Cover photo by Karen Almond

these materials and information. Adherence to all applicable laws and regulations, both advertising and all other aspects of doing business in the United States or any other jurisdiction, is the sole responsibility of the purchaser or reader.

This book is intended to provide accurate information with regard to the subject matter covered. However, the Author and the Publisher accept no responsibility for inaccuracies or omissions, and the Author and Publisher specifically disclaim any liability, loss, or risk, whether personal, financial, or otherwise, that is incurred as a consequence, directly or indirectly, from the use and/or application of any of the contents of this book.

This book is dedicated to the amazing women who have informed, enriched, enlightened, and enhanced my life.

Table of Contents

Foreword

Margery Miller has written a deeply personal and practical guide to being true to yourself and your values. She is my coach, dear friend, sister, and now the author of Great Girls Network Series: *Confessions of a Recovering Helpaholic.*

I met Margery in her hometown of Dallas in 2005 at a women's leadership conference. She spoke to me right after I had launched the first Make Mine a Million $ Business competition and generously offered to help me. These are words you truly hope to hear when you have just launched something incredible and overwhelming.

How she thought she could help me the most was to coach me in the development of the Make Mine a Million $ Business program. Margery's vast experience as a successful woman business owner and as a seasoned business and life coach helped enormously. Dozens of women quickly grew their micro businesses to million-dollar enterprises with her guidance, and the program grew from a pilot to a roaring success on the journey to women's economic independence.

She taught me that to grow your business, you have to grow yourself. Through my own successes and failures, divorce, death of loved ones, shame and triumph, I have been growing myself while listening to her. She and I continue our conversation as we both branch out into new ventures, some together, some separately.

Margery lives life out loud, describing what she sees and expressing how she feels. This book from the Great Girls Network Series: *Confessions of a Recovering Helpaholic* is the first of what I hope will be many volumes of practical brilliance that she shares with the world.

Consider yourself lucky to have crossed paths with Margery in print or in person. Your life will never be the same. I am deeply grateful for all that I have learned from her.

~ Nell Merlino

Nell Merlino is an award-winning activist and advocate for women and girls. She mobilized millions of people to recognize girls' potential with **Take Our Daughters to Work Day.** She launched **Count Me In for Women's Economic Independence** to inspire women's economic empowerment in 2000. With Hillary Clinton's support, Nell launched the **Make Mine a Million $ Business** program, helping women grow micro businesses to million-dollar companies. Nell has provided commentary to every major news outlet across the United States, generating over three billion media mentions about the progress of women and girls. She is the author of ***Stepping Out of Line: Lessons for Women Who Want it Their Way in Life, in Love, and at Work*** (available on Amazon) and **"Cracking the Glass Ceiling and Raising the Roof"** in *MIT Innovations Journal*, Winter/Spring 2013.

Foreword

Part 1

Becoming a Great Girl

I write this from a lifetime of experience that has led me here. The truth is, I believe we are **all** born Great Girls. The problem is our awareness of it. Here's how my awareness developed:

I grew up in Dallas, Texas, the daughter of a first generation Russian Jewish immigrant and an east Texas Baptist who met each other, fell in love during the WWII years, got married, and had four daughters within five years. They were young, pretty clueless about raising kids (as most people were in the late '40s, early '50s), and did the best they could.

The good thing is that I wasn't force-fed a religion because my parents didn't decide what to guide us toward until my older sister wanted to be fully Jewish, and we went to classes at our local temple. It didn't impact my life very much because, for some reason, I already felt a spiritual sense of life and had come to the conclusion that God is inside us. That set me free to become a true seeker later in life.

My sisters and I were punished if my parents caught us fighting, so we didn't develop what I now understand to be healthy relationship skills of conflict resolution. That has been a lifelong challenge for me, one that led me to an abiding interest in human behavior. I felt alone and separate from the others in my family, as I imagine most kids did during that time.

As a teenager, I became engulfed in theater and studied drama avidly. It took me out of the family and into my own world. I loved it so much, I was determined to become a musical comedy actor on Broadway. That dream was destroyed when, home from college in California during my freshman year, I went on a blind date and he, unbeknownst to me, had drunk too much and drove us into a light post. My right foot was ripped off to the side, my right arm broken, my back injured. It took six months to recover enough to walk and return to summer school, more surgeries on my foot, and an attempt to continue to study drama at SMU in Dallas. My parents caught me having sex with my boyfriend (I was 19) over spring break and decided I had violated the "family honor" and excommunicated me from my family and told me they would no longer be willing to send me to an expensive private university. They told me I had to leave my beloved drama program at SMU and go to a state school.

Instead, I left home, wandered around staying with friends until I got scared and realized I didn't know what I was doing. I hooked up with a guy I sort of knew from SMU who was madly in love with me and wanted to get married. I figured it was a better option than wandering the streets, so I said yes.

Back then (1967), you were considered an old maid spinster if you weren't married by your early 20s. It was common for women to think the most important thing they could get from college was an "MRS Degree," so I imagine my parents decided that if I got married, I would somehow be safe and settled. They gave me a lovely wedding.

Little did they know that their actions would lead to me become the opposite of what they wanted. The guy I married was a radical thinker who wrote for a newspaper called *Notes from the Underground*, and after six months of him deciding that he needed to be involved full time in The Movement (against the war in Viet Nam and for opening admissions to black people in colleges and universities, along with free speech), we both quit our jobs, lived in an old car, and traveled Texas and Oklahoma setting up Students for a Democratic Society (SDS) chapters. I had gradually become politicized over the preceding years, and it felt like the right thing to do.

By March of 1969, after a year and a half of marriage, it was clearly not working for us. He moved to Houston; I left and moved to NYC to be with new friends with whom I had connected in The

Movement. A speech I'd made at a rally held at the University of Houston turned out to have led to some damages at the student center, and months later, I was arrested by the FBI in Chicago while attending a national SDS convention for an incitement to riot charge in Texas. I managed to get help from radical lawyers in Chicago and ended up staying there on probation until the leader of the Black Panther Party was murdered there, which caused me to flip out emotionally and led me on a journey of questions with no answers and ultimately to a commune in Vermont. After five months of living truly in tents in the woods, I realized that the guy who owned the land got to make all the decisions, didn't feel like I belonged there, and hooked up with a young guy I met from a local college and lived with him for a few months after I found out the FBI was looking for me for jumping my probation in Chicago.

With advice from a radical lawyer, I decided to contact my parents and return to Texas to resolve my legal issues. I got home at the end of November, and fortunately, my parents decided to help me. The situation really changed when I realized I was pregnant. I thought seriously about getting an abortion but just couldn't do it. So here was my situation: still legally married to a guy in Houston (by now a known, and considered dangerous, radical who I hadn't seen in almost two years); pregnant by someone else; needing to **not** go to jail; unemployed.

I came out of it okay – got a fine from an understanding judge, got a divorce with the help of a family friend's law firm, and found Montessori education and an opportunity to go to Mexico to study for two years with my baby.

From there, it seemed like my life sped by. After getting my Montessori teaching degree, I returned to Texas, met someone new, and thought I could create a whole new life unrelated to before. And… have a father for my child. It was now 1974, and my naïve self thought getting married again was a good move. As you will learn later in this book, not so much; however, it was part of my journey and very much a blessing though also a devastating challenge.

That marriage led me to become a business woman and combine all the skills I had developed through the years to support myself into a unique understanding of how to build successful businesses. I utilized the secretarial skills I learned on jobs I took during my early 20s (to survive the radical years), I used the depth of understanding of what people need in my Montessori education, and the beautiful teachings of all the spiritual studies I undertook starting in 1970 (and continue to this day) to try to help me make some sense of the world we live in.

After my second marriage failed, I got scared again and remarried a third time, too quickly, and got out of it seven months later. By age 42, I became well aware that marriages were *not* a viable option for me, as I obviously had (and still seem to have) a "bad picker." I have had many relationships with men since then, all of which taught me wonderful lessons and kept me walking my path alone, as far as a companion is concerned.

Where I am *not* alone is why this book exists. I am now and have for years been a part of my own "great girls network." I have amassed, from around the world, an ever-expanding circle of female friends who have challenged and supported me at every step of my journey. Some have become part of my past, yet I still value their contributions to my life.

The lessons I have learned are included in this book. My experiences have been my teachers, and I am so grateful for the women *and men* who have both wittingly and unwittingly participated in them.

I started the Great Girls Network because the "good ol' boy network" is so alive and well that I believe we need to have an antithesis for it. Maybe that is endemic to Texas, but I see the "power of patriarchy" around the world, no matter what you call it, and women have been subjected to it throughout history.

I believe it is time for women to truly stand up and speak up. I am dedicated to helping women find their inner voices, reach out to each other, and work together to keep changing our world.

In that respect, although these are "confessions of a recovering helpaholic," in actuality, I am hoping to enable other women to become adept at offering and giving help to each other (and truly, all humanity) that doesn't boomerang back on them and cause them more pain.

The lessons in this book are how I learned to do that, to take really good care of myself, and keep helping others in a healthy, productive way. I hope that it inspires you to do the same.

Facing Yourself

This book is a play on looking at whatever we do that we can't seem to stop as an addiction. Yes, I am fully aware that the severity of "helpaholism" doesn't equal the devastating consequences of drug or alcohol addiction; however, it does have a serious effect on our lives. We put ourselves into situations that don't work for us and don't seem to have the awareness or the ability to change the behavior.

I realized after writing the first six steps of my 12-Step Program for Recovering Helpaholics that it is sort of divided into two parts. The beginning steps (1-

6) are about facing ourselves. The next group (7-12) is about healing ourselves.

These steps come from my years of coaching (45!) and my journey of self-discovery, self-improvement, and all the incredibly challenging yet beneficial experiences that have kept me focused on my inner growth. I write this as much for myself as for others, as I need encouragement just like everyone else!

Chapter 1:

What Exactly Is a Helpaholic?

If an alcoholic sees a drink, she might just drink it....

If a foodaholic sees food, she might just eat it....

When a helpaholic sees someone who needs something, her first response is usually, "How can I help?"

Oh, you say, "Isn't that a good thing? Wanting to help others?"

"Maybe... maybe not!"

Did the person ask for help? Did the two of you establish some ground rules, some boundaries before the help was given?

Or did it all happen so fast that you look up and realize you're in the middle of something and starting to feel like, "Uh-oh, I've done it again"?

As I am now the glorious age of 71, I find myself reassessing how I go about living. I truly feel young (I keep saying I feel like a 70-year-old child!),

and I expect to live quite a few more years. I don't want to keep repeating behavior that makes me feel foolish, gullible, tired, frustrated, drained, spent, sad, and well, just plain miserable.

This has been a year of tremendous change for me. My friend, Lida says I am cleansing. It is actually a soul cleansing – similar to when you change your diet and your body starts to realign itself. I am clearing out old habits – old patterns that are not going to lead me where I want to go.

I want to be one of those 90-year-old women who still drive around and do their own shopping, have great friends and fulfilling activities. But if I keep getting myself into situations in which I feel stressed out, sad, frustrated, and impotent – that isn't going to happen!

How can you know you're a helpaholic?

How often do you feel stressed out, sad, frustrated, and impotent? Not that momentary thing that happens with situations that go south on you. No, I'm talking about an underlying feeling that drains your energy and has you repeating things over and over. Like explaining to someone why you're upset (again). Like hoping this time it will be different (again). Like trying so hard and feeling like it boomerangs on you. That feeling.

Not too different from, "I have my drinking under control, so I'll just have this one glass of wine (and then another, and another…)." Or, I'll just eat a couple of cookies (then eat the whole bag…). Or I'll just place this one bet…. You get the idea, right?

So we see someone who we think needs our help and, before they even ask for it, we're coming up with great ideas, strategies, new ways to solve the problem – their problem. *Before they even ask for it!* Because we're sure they need the help. It just comes naturally to us. We can't seem to *help* it!

> *The problem with us helpaholics is that we are as sneaky and self-deluded as any other "holic" — we convince ourselves that we really are happy doing what we're doing!*

And then we set about convincing them, swooping in to start helping, letting them know we're there for them. We're so generous! Kind-hearted! Understanding! Someone they can count on!

And our ideas are really good… we're sure of it!

Being generous has its own reward, right?

Oh, yes. We get rewarded all right. We get to feel valuable. Until we wake up and realize that they

17

aren't there for us in the same way. We have taught them to enjoy our generosity, our attention, our encouragement. And we get to feel unappreciated, unseen, frustrated, and unimportant.

Because we aren't in fair exchange.

Who's the priority?

One day while I was exercising, a question popped into my mind: **When am I going to be as important to myself as I make other people?**

At a recent Great Girls Network Track meeting, we were reminded of Maya Angelou's quote: "Never make someone a priority when all you are to them is an option."

> *I feel like a priority when I am a priority to myself.*

I have had to face that more times than I want to admit! I project my picture of what is important out into the world, not realizing that others' priorities do not come close to matching mine. So I'm changing the way I connect with people. I ask myself what works for me – *first*! It doesn't mean I don't also make an effort to be accommodating to other people; I just don't accommodate them before I figure out what works for me.

What will it take to break this pattern?

I figure if other "holics" need 12-step programs, then we helpaholics do, too.

Step 1: Add a little cynicism to your life. Learn to ask the question: What's in it for me?

That doesn't mean stop helping others completely. It means, look for some form of fair exchange before you do it. And stop being so naïve! Look at the helping opportunity as a win-win for both of you.

- Does it make your friendship stronger?
- Are you building a true relationship?
- Are you giving more than you are getting?
- Are you doing things and *hoping* they appreciate it?
- Is there some form of reciprocation?
- Is helping actually your secret strategy to feeling liked by others?

I started this journey on the road to helpaholic recovery as a blog because I know I need to face the dark part of myself that gets me into situations that don't feel good. It starts with a confession... because I want to heal my way out of this, not blame someone else for it.

To put it bluntly, I have consistently gotten myself into situations in which I felt used. And I can't blame the person I have been helping, because I wasn't taking care of myself – that's my responsibility, not theirs.

> *Facing myself is the first step on the road to recovery.*

I was born a pleaser. I like to do things for people. It feels good. Until it doesn't!

Chapter 2:

Who's Responsible?

When I initially wrote this as a blog, my mind worked overtime after I wrote the first step. I really wanted to get to Steps 2 and 3 of my 12-Step program. Then I realized I just needed to let it come to me, through conversations and experiences.

Now that being a helpaholic has become a major topic of discussion with my friends and clients, I see more each day just how insidious this addiction is! So I took my time thinking about and writing the first five steps, and I was sure the rest would come to me in the same way.

Step 2: Stop taking responsibility for other people's experiences.

When I coach clients, I am able to have a detached perspective. They pay me to work with them, then it is up to them to utilize what they learn and do something about it. In that area, I have no problem with "over-involvement."

On a personal basis, with friends and family, it took me a while to realize I was doing this, then more time to figure out why and what it was doing to me. What came to me was this:

When I would offer to help someone, along with that help came an unconscious attachment to the outcome. When I did the *Strengths Finder*, a test devised by Marcus Buckingham and Donald O. Clifton and shared in their book, *Now, Discover Your Strengths,*, I found my Signature Themes were Activator (make things happen), Maximizer (stimulating excellence), Strategic (create alternative ways to proceed), Relator (work hard with friends to achieve a goal) and Futuristic (inspired by the future and what could be).

I now see those are a perfect combination to encourage my helpaholism! Once I became unconsciously attached to an outcome, I would work feverishly to try to make it happen. Instead of just offering suggestions or providing a reasonable amount of assistance, I would dive in and get way too involved

> *Helpaholics become overly attached to the outcome.*

emotionally in solving the problem, or at least working on the solution.

Isn't working on a solution a good thing?

Yes and no. It depends on how much attachment or detachment you have. A detached form of help is: I see you have some options, which are _____, so I hope you figure it out. Let me know how it goes.

An attached form of help is: I see you have some options, which are _____, so let me figure out how to make those happen, and keep me posted on your progress, so I can stay involved and make sure it happens!

Even when you brainstorm and help figure out a strategy, your job doesn't then become *execution*. That is their responsibility, not yours!

If you're working on a team, then each person has a share in the strategy and the outcome. But that is different from what I'm talking about here.

Okay, I get it. Stop getting too involved in other people's strategies and outcomes. Is that it?

Not quite. There is another form of taking responsibility for other people's experiences: when we think they need our intervention or assistance and they haven't even asked for it.

Say you witness your sister fighting with her husband. You have all kinds of ideas about how they could work it out, so you offer to help.

Did they (or she) ask you? Were you invited to that little party or are you trying to crash it? Of course you're not seeing yourself as a party crasher – just a loving, helpful sister, right? Wrong! Especially with family members, but really, as a rule, I find that unless I am asked, my help really isn't welcome.

The thing to ask yourself is this: Why am I trying to help? Is this my way of feeling connected, like I belong? Is this my childhood pattern? Helping can be the way you feel connected to others. For me, I have had to face that I developed the "helpful" behavior to win the approval of others. I felt isolated and alone (even though I had three sisters!) as a child. I can see that I started helping to gain acceptance and a sense of belonging. And that strategy wasn't bad – it actually worked for me for quite a while.

But I'm not a child anymore; I'm ready to have a different life. I'm only 71! I have maybe 20 more great years ahead. So I'm working on breaking patterns that don't work for me anymore. And being too helpful, getting all entangled in other people's situations where I don't actually belong... that just isn't working for me anymore!

Chapter 3:

How You Treat Yourself Matters

Breaking old patterns came up in the last chapter, and I have to admit I am probably harder on myself than anyone else when I catch myself repeating behavior that I have committed to changing. This is where I saw the need for Step 3:

Step 3: Be kinder to yourself!

Many of us who care about personal development are our own worst critics because we keep thinking we aren't making changes fast enough – or learning what we need to learn soon enough! Years ago, I had a client in her mid-50s tell me how angry she was because she "should have been finished working on herself by now...." I calmly explained that working on ourselves is a lifelong journey, and it was unrealistic to think at her relatively young age she would be "done" by now.

She didn't like my response… and didn't keep coming to see me. Which was okay with me – because I knew even then that it would have been an uphill battle to keep trying to help her when she wasn't actually open to ongoing personal growth.

Not everyone is. As I have gotten older, it has become very clear to me that I resonate with some people, and I don't with others. And that is fine with me because then I don't have to get that scrunchy feeling in my face and that tense feeling in my head and shoulders when I keep trying to communicate with people who are simply not on the same page with me.

It doesn't mean they are wrong. For them, their lives are working just fine. Or as fine as they want things at that moment.

That is one way I have learned to be kinder to myself. No one can be all things to all people, so trying to help others see or understand how things could be different can actually be a losing battle which just makes us feel, once again, depleted!

When do you know it is time to let go?

That probably varies with different situations, mainly when it is something you feel that you have given enough effort toward and it just isn't happening. One thing I am *really* working on is the notion that if I explain it another way, use different examples, they will "get it" – when that isn't a truly possible outcome and I just don't want to face it.

> *If they don't "get it," move on.*

It's that adage, "If a door doesn't open, maybe it's the wrong door" (paraphrased), but you get what I mean.

So I need to be kinder to myself regarding communication with others. Is that it?

Not quite. The other part is how we view ourselves. I realize even more than being hard on myself by making too much effort to help others, I can so easily slip into self-critical mode thinking I "should" be doing more – more writing, more exercising, more cooking, more whatever!

We all have a standard to which we hold ourselves accountable. I think my habit is to pretty much do what I want each day, then give myself a hard time because I didn't meet the much higher standard I imagine I ought to be living up to.

Why? It's probably a leftover from childhood when I didn't think I measured up. I wasn't as smart as my older sister. I wasn't as cute as my friends. I didn't get the part I wanted in the school play because someone else was "better" than I was.... I can name so many ways I felt "less than" as a kid, and the frustration about those experiences seems to have implanted itself into my cellular memory.

I see this pattern slowly unraveling, but it still crops up. So I have to regroup, have a serious talk with myself – or if I'm too far down the rabbit hole of self-flagellation, I call one of my closest friends and get some help.

Does that work?

Actually, it does. At least it helps me get back to center. Most of my friends admit that we are all harder on ourselves than we are on others. My goal is to catch it as soon as possible and reverse the downward spiral. Thank goodness I have friends to help me!

Chapter 4:

We All Need Limits

One of the areas we helpaholics get caught up in is *family*. Invariably there are one, maybe two people in any given family who seem to have an uber sense of responsibility toward the family as a whole and whether they stay connected, get along, etc.

Which brings me to our next step:

Step 4: Set clear boundaries with family members.

It took me so long to learn this!

We used to call our mother "the benevolent dictator." She looked and acted like the sweetest person ever, but when she wanted something done, she was masterful at getting her daughters to cooperate. Well, a couple of daughters anyway. My youngest sister, Diann, and I were the ones who were the family people. My two other sisters... not so much.

If I tried to talk to my mother about things between me and my sisters that weren't working, she would say, "I'm not going to discuss that." Which translated to me: "Suck it up; we don't talk about feelings in this house."

So I spent the better part of the last 60-something years letting things slide as I dutifully went about arranging holiday dinners, staying in contact with my sisters about whatever was going on with our parents (especially during the 20 years of their failing health), and keeping the peace by keeping my mouth shut as much as possible.

My dad died in 2006, and I spent the next 10 years being my mother's "person" – and we actually connected on a much deeper level than ever possible during the "nuclear family" years. I learned to be direct and honest with her, and when she would give me those "don't you go there" looks, I simply plowed ahead anyway and helped her face her own stuff about the way she treated me. I was just tired of being criticized and demeaned because of her habit of speaking to me. And glory be... she actually changed! She became more honest and less manipulative. We became good friends.

That friendship bled into her relationships with my other sisters to a degree, although I don't really know how close they felt to each other because, by then, I figured it wasn't my responsibility to keep fueling the fires, so to speak.

And now your boundaries with your sisters are clear?

Not exactly. I had to learn a very bitter lesson about that right after my mother's memorial service. My older sister had been staying with me (she lives in California) when she would come to visit our mom, and we actually took some trips together during the last several years of mom's life. I had gotten great at being clear with our mother; because we spent so much time together, it was actually a necessity!

My sister came infrequently, and at most we saw each other maybe three times a year. With her, I had such a habit of putting up with attitudes and behaviors that I didn't really appreciate that I just kept doing it – not speaking up, not letting her know I was frustrated with her. I slipped into the family pattern of keeping the peace, usually at all costs.

After the service, as I drove her to the airport, the dam finally burst and I started telling her things that I was uncomfortable about, that bothered me. I tried to explain that I wasn't trying to break our relationship; I was actually trying to build it to be more honest and thereby stronger.

The result was a complete blow up and what seemed to be the end of whatever friendship we had. She was so angry and hurt. After she got back home, a month or so later, I tried again to talk to her, which resulted in a very unpleasant shouting response from her.

I can fully understand why she was so angry. She was horrified that I had not been honest with her in all the years up to that point. And she was right! It was a passive aggressive move on my part – even though I didn't see it at the time.

I don't know if we will ever be able to create an actual friendship.

Setting boundaries means being honest... and doing it as soon as possible!

My wrong was to keep my mouth shut for so long. And it isn't even a problem that I have with people in my daily life. We have great give and take, and don't feel uncomfortable telling the truth about what works and doesn't work for us.

> *Honest boundaries helped me overcome deeply etched patterns.*

But with my sisters, because the family pattern was so deeply etched into me, I kept my distance and kept the peace – which turned out to be war when the truth finally came out.

My third sister doesn't have any problem lashing out at me to tell me all the things she holds against me – and it actually helps because it is clear to me that we have no reason to hang out together. If I run across her or spend time around her due to family circumstances, I am careful to steer clear of any alone time with her. I appreciate knowing how she really feels about me because I don't feel compelled to make something happen. It sets me free! We didn't have the closer connection that I had with my older sister, so I don't miss anything.

With my older sister, I miss the connection. We do communicate by email from time to time, very polite, passing information about the dismantling of my mother's estate (for which I'm the executrix). So possibly enough time will pass that we will simply start over, or something like that.

I'm grateful that I am still deeply connected to Diann, who has definitely moved into the family of choice category. We have somehow managed to be honest and forthright with each other for years. And we really enjoy each other!

So do you think it is all right, not to be close with all your family?

For me, that depends on what family you're talking about. I am very close with my family of choice – the people I have built deep, fulfilling relationships with over my adult life. I can't imagine my life without them! I rely on them for all the challenge and support that true friendship provides.

So the point I'm really making here is this: Family, after you grow up, is a state of mind, not an obligation. Where we come from is important, but it is more important to be here, today, relating to and connecting with the people who make a positive difference in our lives, even during times we disagree or weather difficulties.

I think redefining our concept of family is the key.

Chapter 5:

Who's in Control?

It's the end of July in Texas and we've had so many days of 100°+ weather that we're all about to wilt! Until today, which started off dark and still, and then it actually rained! Which cooled things off, but reminded me of how dark this next step is...

Step 5: Remember that help is the happy side of control!

Dark you ask? Why?

I think it is probably endemic to human nature to want to control things around us. But what happens when someone calls me a "control freak"? I get defensive! I don't want to be seen that way.

So it pains me to admit that all my helpfulness really does smack of me wanting to be in control. And that is a way of owning my dark side... more than I feel really comfortable doing.

Those of us who love helping (yes, helpaholics!) aren't just doing it altruistically. The hidden motive is to control – if not the person, then perhaps the outcome.

Think about the parent who consistently steps in to "help" the child do things the "right" way. I'm not talking about when the child comes and asks for specific help. I'm talking about the all-knowing parent who observes the child's attempt at something and jumps in to make sure they get it done.

Or the wife or husband who offers to help with a project and before you know it, the project no longer belongs to you. You're being told how to do it, then consistently asked about the results.

Or the friend who can't stop offering advice. And then gets frustrated when the advice isn't followed.

Do you recognize anyone here? It saddens me to say I do. Me!

It's not something I do all the time, but I have to pay close attention to myself not to do it. And I'm grateful to say that my hyper-vigilance is proving fruitful. Especially in the area of communicating with family and friends, I have made great improvement.

Which has resulted in me being more relaxed around them, and us actually getting along better! What a concept!

Isn't this the same thing as not taking responsibility for other people's experiences?

Not quite. With that step, we are making up a story that they need us to take care of them when they haven't asked for it. This type of intervention is different. This is about taking over when they ask for help, or we assume they need our help because of the role we play in their lives. Like a parent, or a teacher, or an employer, in some way we feel we need to exert an authoritative influence. Because we are somehow "experts."

See why I said it feels like I'm baring my dark side? I don't want to be that way with people! Because it has dire consequences:

- My son doesn't want to talk with me when I do it.
- My friends tell me I act like I'm the smartest person in the room (ouch!).
- A spouse with an overbearing mate tends to shrivel and shrink because it is so hard to push against that behavior. (I've had that reaction to overbearing

men – so it is doubly awful if I'm the pushy one!)

- Kids with an overbearing parent could act out their frustration either by rebelling and being angry or cowering and developing extreme anxiety. (I've seen it go both ways.)
- People who are constantly treated as if they are "less than," inferior, or lacking skills tend to accept that identity – especially if it comes from a superior (a boss, a parent, etc.).

Does that mean it is our fault if they react that way?

Not completely. They have the responsibility to look within and make some decisions about themselves: that they are worthy, that they are capable, that they don't have to put up with overbearing people. But why exacerbate their problem? Why not take a step back and let them find out how capable they are on their own?

I know from my many years of study of human behavior that every challenge has a benefit. So when we challenge people by our inappropriate behavior, it doesn't spell ruin for them. They can find a way to stand up to us, to fight for themselves.

I just like myself a lot better when I'm not making things more difficult for people than they already are. Especially if doing it is something I can control!

Who's in Control?

Chapter 6:

Self-Delusion

I took a little time to write this in my mind before setting words down because it is such a personal journey for me to face these dark parts of myself. Yet I find that by owning them out loud, so to speak, and writing about them, it really helps me clear my path toward a more rewarding life experience. The stories that follow are just a tiny few of the times I have had to learn this the hard way. And of course, the cosmic joke on me is that I'm much better at spotting the pattern in others and helping them break it than I have been with myself. Oh, well. At least I keep working on it!

Step 6: Stop thinking, "With me, it will be different!"

Why do I consider that a dark part of myself? Because it makes my tendency for self-delusion public!

Way too many times I have turned off my sweet inner voice – whether it was shouting "danger" or just whispering to me that this situation doesn't feel right. Instead, I have plowed into situations, relationships, difficulties as if I somehow had a secret weapon of invincibility unlike anyone else.

Example:

I start dating someone. He is charming, delightful, interesting. And he also doesn't show up on time, leaves me waiting patiently without even a phone call. Doesn't do things he says he will do. Instead of calling a halt right at the beginning, I make up a story: Once we are really connected, he will see that I am important; he will value me like I want to be valued.

BONG: WRONG ANSWER!!!

He has shown me from the beginning who he is, but I didn't want to see it. I liked my story better. Result: disappointment and eventual end of our connection when I finally decided I was important enough to stop seeing him and subjecting myself to that.

Example:

I hire a new sales person. He doesn't come up with a sales plan from the get go. He has excuses for why things aren't going well. But he comes from a company that was successful, he has a good reputation in our industry (people like him), and I think once he gets the hang of our system, once he realizes what a great company we are to work for, he'll come around. I work on this for over a year, try to get the other sales people to help him, I encourage him, lots of pep talks.

BONG: WRONG ANSWER!!!

Not only does he not improve, he gets worse and worse. I realize he is drinking during lunch breaks. He hangs around the office more than he goes out to make calls. His sales don't ever reach an acceptable level. I end up firing him, and he files for unemployment and I have to explain to the Texas Workforce Commission just why he doesn't deserve it. I won the case, but it was an ugly, unpleasant thing for everyone concerned.

Example:

I married an alcoholic. I didn't want to face that truth and had plenty of ways to avoid it because, in the early '70s, most of my peer group drank, our parents all drank, parties almost always had full bars;

it was our lifestyle. I was madly in love with him. He was handsome; something about being around him soothed me. He was going to be an adoptive father to my son, who was not quite 3-years-old at the time. I was going to have a new life! I eventually quit teaching Montessori and went into the family business to help file invoices. Soon, I realized he wasn't capable of running the business (his dad quickly retired after I showed up), and I started teaching myself how to do what needed to be done. I built a very successful business for my husband and found myself covering for him more and more.

He was unreliable. He didn't show up on time. He would give me that "sh-t-eating grin" which was supposed to charm me back into cooperating and taking care of him. His dad died and he really lost it, started drinking more and more, made bad business decisions that I had to repair. I kept having to tell people that I would solve the problem, that I would get them the information quickly, whatever I needed to do to stop the disaster. I called myself a traveling basketball hoop – anywhere I needed to be, I made sure I was there.

I let my son live in a bad relationship with him. I watched him blow up at my son and sometimes scare him. I kept trying to fix the situation. I got us counseling; I sought help. I felt I was so entwined in the business with him that there were no possible exit strategies. I gained weight. I tried to keep everything going. I stayed married to him for 14 years!

I kept trying to convince myself that he would see the light and change.

BONG: WRONG ANSWER!!!

I filed for divorce to try to scare him to stop drinking. Instead, I found out he had been having affairs with my two saleswomen for the past two years. I went through with the divorce, and he actually quit drinking, but I didn't trust him so I wouldn't take him back. Within nine months, he convinced me to buy him out of the business, which I did. Then I had to deal with all the factories we represented questioning my ability to run the very business I had built and been running all those years because I had let them think that he was far more valuable to it than he actually was. We pulled through it, and I continued running and building it for 18 more years until I sold it to two of my sales guys. It took years for my son to move through his anger about his dad. To this day, this guy sends Christmas presents to my son but has visited him only one time, rarely contacts him. The father I thought I was giving my son was useless to both of us.

Does it sound like it takes me a while to learn my lessons?

Yes it does! And I finally have reconciled myself to a lifelong journey of learning. I fully expect to have many more lessons in the future… because I will continue to "try to do the right thing" and very likely find out the hard way something I needed to learn.

People show us who they are. It is our job to believe them!

My commitment to myself:

- Ask more questions.
- Pay attention to whether they do what they say they will do.
- Notice how they treat others.
- Take more time to really get to know them.
- Once certain behavior patterns are revealed, stop making up stories about how I can influence them to be different.
- Remember the adage: looks like a duck, quacks like a duck, walks like a duck – it's a duck. Stop pretending a swan will somehow magically show up!

Isn't it possible for people to change?

Of course it is! But it is *their* job to do it, not our job to convince them to. If they decide to do the work, show up differently, then I am open to get to know the new, improved version. I'm just letting go of the fantasy that I had anything to do with it, save maybe having been an example of a different way of being.

That is what sets me free.

Self-Delusion

Part 2
Healing Yourself

I hope you are allowing yourself some time to digest new realizations. For me, the Facing Myself part stays in the now because I can't imagine not continuing to run into "learning opportunities" for the rest of my life.

In this next section, I'm sharing things I have learned from others and from my own experiences. I'm hoping that you will also continue to seek assistance from myriad corners along your life journey.

Years ago, I realized we are all pilgrims on the path. Sometimes we reach back to offer a helping hand to someone. Later we reach up to get some help. For me, it can easily be the same person. I have cultivated a large circle of people in my life who are as much my teachers as they are my students. Without them, I might still be stuck in some really bad places!

Part 2: Healing Yourself

Chapter 7:

It's Hard to Wait

As I shared at the start, I write this as much for myself as for others, as I need encouragement just like everyone else!

Which leads me to:

Step 7: Learn the art of proactive waiting.

So often we are in a situation that seems utterly beyond our control. Waiting for a decision from someone else. Waiting for someone to do something they said they would do. Waiting, waiting, waiting.

That can make me crazy!

I want things to happen when I want them to happen.

So I came up with a way to manage those moments without losing my mind: proactive waiting.

Example:

We started taking memberships for Great Girls Network in May 2017. We had done our research, determined a reasonable fee for a yearly cost, surveyed women to find out what they wanted from us, and then put out the call to join. And waited.

Not fun to wait! We, of course, knew what a great thing we had! We wanted other women to know also. But it takes time to build things. People had a lot on their plates. They're busy!

While we waited, we started doing Track meetings. These came from the request of the women who had been attending our semi-annual gatherings since 2014. They loved getting together with women they might not meet otherwise, but they felt the groups were too large for more intimate, meaningful conversations. In our surveys, we asked them to choose from several topics the smaller meetings could cover. From that input, we tried four different ones at first, and only two of them, Growth and Transitions really took off. So we stayed with them. Gradually, the word got out and we kept attracting new members. We just kept going, enjoying each smaller gathering, learning

> *I've learned there is benefit in proactive waiting.*

about ourselves along the way. Later in 2017, we added a third one, Be Well.

What I find most interesting is that at this point, after well over a year of Track meetings, we continue to evolve as a group. The women who joined in the beginning but didn't actually connect with us have started dropping away. And at the same time, we are attracting new members who resonate with what we're about.

What is evident is that we are really about encouraging each other to speak our truth, be vulnerable, appreciate ourselves and each other. Some women don't find that compelling. And that is okay! We can't be all things to all people.

For those of us who like that, it works. We have a very strong core group, who come often to Track meetings. Growing that is most important to us.

And we are fine proactively waiting for others to connect!

Example:

When I was running my manufacturers' sales agency (1977 to 2006), we were often approached by companies with a possibility of being chosen to represent them. Very few of those were cut-and-dried decisions because many factors entered into them: who else we represented, who currently had (or had just lost) the line, how big our reach was in the particular market segment they wanted serviced. Sometimes, it would take a few months before a decision was made. If it was a line we really wanted, it was a bit agonizing to wait until hearing the result. Difficult!

We had to put the decision aside and move on with our sales efforts with the lines we already had, giving it our all. We learned to not ever bank on it going our way, and especially to not talk about it with others... for several reasons. The current reps might plead their case to keep the line. Another company might swoop in to compete with us if they knew the line was available. A customer might try to sway the company to go with a favorite rep group (not us) instead. How did we learn this? The hard way, of course! By saying the wrong thing to the wrong person at the wrong time!

What was originally a protective move, to keep quiet and keep working, turned out to be highly beneficial. We just kept getting stronger, more reliable and more experienced in making the sales for our current factories, and it gave us a much better chance to earn new lines for the future. It also kept us from the highs and lows of false expectations and the inevitable disappointment if it didn't go in our favor.

That strategy obviously worked well: The guys I sold my business to 12 years ago are still going strong, still building a successful company! And I'm really pleased to have been part of that.

Example:

This next one was hard for me to learn. Someone told me recently that I seem to be very patient with others. I think I actually do that to a fault sometimes. Especially with men. I was raised in a culture that made men the center of the world. When I grew up in the '50s, the highlight of the day was when Daddy came home. We got him a drink, rubbed his feet (he was a surgeon, on his feet a lot during the day), and made sure he had the best of everything. It was a societal norm.

It took me years to understand that catering to men was not actually working for me. Sure, I was good at running my business, running my life on the outside. But when it came to relationships, I found myself slipping into patterns that left me out in the cold. If a guy was late, I made it all right. If he didn't do what he said he would do, I worked around it. I was a master at making life better for the men I cared about.

How does proactive waiting apply to this?

I no longer put men above me in any way. I stop seeing a guy if he shows me he doesn't consider me a priority. I have clear boundaries.

And I don't have a boyfriend, and that is fine with me! I am building and enjoying a wonderful life. I have the best friends (both male and female) you could imagine. I have fun. I do what I love! I don't feel a lack in my life because there isn't a man to share it.

I am proactively waiting for a really cool, aware guy who gets that hanging out with me is a great thing. And if he doesn't show up in this lifetime, I still have a great life! And my heart belongs to me.

Chapter 8:

You Just Can't Know

This is about living in the unknown. For as long as I've been coaching people, I have had to field their questions about what will happen next. We can make up stories about what we think will happen. What we want to happen. What we hope will happen. But we cannot possibly know.

Which leads us to:

Step 8: Learn to live in the Fertile Void.

Say you're going to plant a garden. You map out a plot of land. You till the soil, prepare it for planting. You make your rows and neatly put your seeds or seedlings in the ground. Then you wait.

Depending on what you plant, it could take weeks or even longer before anything shows up.

If you get anxious and start digging around to see if the seeds are growing, you will destroy all the little root hairs that are starting to form. Then your garden is ruined, and you have to start over or give up. So instead, you wait, but waiting doesn't guarantee that what you thought you planted will show up in the way you thought it would. The seeds could have been mixed up. You might end up with purple flowers when you thought you planted red ones!

That is the Fertile Void.

Your life is similar to that garden. You have great ideas, hopes, and dreams. You plant seeds to bring them to fruition. And sometimes, it gets very frustrating to wait until you see results.

In Step 7, I talked about proactive waiting. For me, that is the only way to manage living in the Fertile Void; however, something needs to be added: trust.

> *With trust, embrace the unknown – the Fertile Void.*

Not knowing and not going crazy requires trust. People get that sense of trust in many ways: trusting God, trusting the Universe, religious beliefs, having faith in others – all engender a sense of trust that things will turn out well. I think the most important place is within ourselves, learning to trust our inner voices.

Example:

Up until a few months ago, I was raising a teenager. It was something that sort of landed in my lap, and I embraced the challenge fully for about four years. This situation stopped working for various reasons last winter, and by the end of March, she determined that she was not going to stay with me. She was 15, so I felt she had the right to make that choice; I didn't fight it.

I had bought a fairly large house to be able to take care of her and her brother at the end of 2014, once we decided to leave the home of her grandfather where we had lived most of that year. Her brother decided to live somewhere else (he was already 15 by then), so she and I moved together. It really worked for a while. We added a housemate and created a sort of family. It fell apart in 2017 when the housemate got pregnant, and I told her I didn't want to help raise a baby, so she moved out. The girl and I lasted another seven months together, but the relationship deteriorated because she wanted no rules, and I wasn't going to accept that.

Now I'm in a big house, living in the up-and-down cycle of one day deciding to sell it and find a smaller place and the next day really liking my space and thinking I could live here for years. I've fixed this house just the way that works for me. But is that the reason to stay here? I just don't know! Part of my difficulty in deciding is that I know deep inside I am still healing from the devastating pain of trying so hard to do the right thing for this girl and for her to walk away from it. I need time to process what happened.

I'm in the Fertile Void. I know that until I really process it, this isn't the time to decide anything. My house is paid for, so all I have is my upkeep. I have help for that, so there is no urgent reason to decide anything. I'm practicing the art of proactive waiting while I'm in the Fertile Void… and trusting that once I know what to do, I will be able to act on it.

Example:

People from around the world have caught on to the idea of Great Girls Network. They want to start a group. I love the idea, and I can imagine an international organization. But I'm not ready to do it.

I'm still healing from the changes of the last few months. I am rebuilding my identity from parent to free woman. I have nothing to tie me to one place except my commitment to the GGN group, and I love holding our Track meetings three Wednesdays a month. I love my friends here; I love all the new people I'm meeting from our Great Girls Network.

I'm trusting that time is on my side, that as I transform myself, I will understand what the next steps are. I am getting help from the women who are also committed to grow our group and feel like we will learn as we go what works and what doesn't work. I call it growing organically. I believe in us. I feel we are growing; I'm just not sure the exact form we will become. Chapters around the world? People who can commit to forming groups? Available spaces? So many unknowns!

So, GGN is in the Fertile Void. I know we're on to something here. I feel the power of connection at each Track meeting, each large gathering. And others are feeling it, too. We have a core group of committed women. It actually feels exciting not to know what is coming because we're on a journey of discovery together. Fun!

Lesson:

For me, the Fertile Void is one of the most important stages of personal development. The two small examples I used are the simplest way I can explain it, but I encourage whoever is reading this to let go of needing to know and embrace not knowing. It is a lesson I learned from reading and working with Angeles Arrien, Ph.D., a cross-cultural anthropologist who wrote *The Four-Fold Way*. In it, she explains the four basic archetypes of the human character from a feminine perspective. In the Teacher chapter, she delves into the propensity of humans to need to know and how that needing to know can be an addiction that gets in the way of meaningful growth. I highly recommend her book.

I'm so grateful to Angeles and all the experiences that have led me to appreciate the Fertile Void.

Chapter 9:

Don't Try to Do It Alone

When I write these chapters (and as I wrote the original blog posts), I realize that I am speaking about things that I have learned from others – my experiences wouldn't mean much if I only had them by myself! This is why my next step is so important:

Step 9: Find a group and learn from them

One of the reasons I started Great Girls Network is that I wanted other women to enjoy the benefits of what had been enriching, expanding, and informing my life since my early 20s: I already had a "great girls network!" I have a panel of experts I can call on around the world.

Some of them are actually men, but they are men who appreciate and support women. Most of them, however, are women. We challenge each other. We support each other. We stand by each other. We learn from each other.

My first and for me most dramatic experience of this was when I was barely 24 years old and I moved, with a 4-week-old baby, to Mexico City to study Montessori education. I was still in a state of recovery from having been involved in The Movement – I had been part of the anti-war effort, among other things in the late '60s, ended up living in a commune in Vermont, and landed back in Texas pregnant and without a future mapped out clearly – as I shared at the beginning of this book.

I got back to Texas and reconnected with a friend from a few years back who had a son in a Montessori school. She introduced me to her friends, one of whom was a teacher there. She introduced me to her mentor, a woman from Holland who was starting a training program with the Mexican government to introduce Montessori to Mexico. I got enveloped by the loving energy, the acceptance of those women, and the feeling that I could maybe

> *Telling this story is bringing the same tears of gratitude that I felt in that moment 47 years ago. I will never forget it.*

make a life for me and my child if I continued my education that way.

My parents agreed to help me, and once my son was born, insisted that I go ahead and leave Dallas to make sure I was at the school when the training program started. Which landed me in a sort of dark and dreary hotel in Polanco, in Mexico City. The stress of travel gave me a breast infection, and I was lying in the bed, trying to figure out what to do. I heard a knock on the door and this dear woman opened it and said, "Hi, I'm Penny, and I've come to see if I can help you."

She was also a student who had come for the training. She was 36; she had children who had stayed behind in Virginia with her ex-husband and his wife, so she could take this course. She understood what my predicament was, helped me find a doctor, get medicine and get better. We bonded at that moment, and even though we went separate ways through the years, I still love her dearly and think of her often. We were friends throughout the training course, and she decided to stay in Mexico

> *She taught me what it means to have women in your life who are not only friends, but mentors, teachers and fun companions on adventures.*

and work with the school, bringing her children down when she could. She introduced me to a study of metaphysics that I followed for another 15 years. She helped me understand what patience looks like, as she seemed to have an infinite amount of it!

She was a conduit to helping me connect with other women at our school (there were 20 Americans and 55 Mexicans attending) and helped me keep my bearings as I juggled raising a baby to a toddler and going to school full time. We spent two years at that school, and I went back to Mexico from time to time to visit her.

Once I moved back to Texas to teach school, the connections with Penny, our friend Marjorie and other Montessori people helped me re-acclimate to my life as a mother and teacher. I met my second husband through a connection with the school, and a year later started my new life as a wife, mother, and teacher. When we moved to Houston for his work, I immediately bonded with my neighbor who was the first person I met on my street. Lida and I have now been best friends for 43 years! She exactly fits the description above and is usually my first "go-to" for counsel, sharing and comfort.

What Lida and I have experienced over those years is probably enough to write several books! And although she lives in Houston, she even joined Great

Girls Network so she attends Track meetings when she comes to visit!

So once I find a group, I'm set, right?

One blessing for me is that I haven't limited myself to only one group.

My Step 9 is a starting point, and I encourage you to use it as a springboard for myriad connections and relationships. I have a group of eight women I have lunch with once a month. We not only celebrate our birthdays, but keep track of life changes, things we're excited about, things we are working on. Those lunches have become a vital part of my life! We all know each other's stuff, and we just pick up where we left off each time – even if we don't make it one month, it is easy to catch up because of our history.

I have a large circle of friends from the days when I was an avid Demartini student. Even though I don't attend the classes anymore, I still have the friends. I have places I can visit and hang with them all over the world!

I have another group of closest friends that started when we all went on a retreat to celebrate a friend's birthday in 2003. We knew each other, some better than others, and that trip launched us into such deep relationships that we truly think of ourselves as sisters. And we challenge each other like sisters! I recently wrote something in an email to the group, and two of them pushed back and let me know they thought I was out of line. I was grateful for the heads up, corrected my error and we all moved on. Who would I be if my friends didn't call me on my stuff? I don't really want to imagine it.

I have many more examples of groups I stay connected with, but you get the point!

So spending a lot of time with friends is the key?

Not quite. The older you get, the more important friends are, and the less time it is necessary to spend with them.

What I am saying here is: Keeping friends isn't about how much time you spend with them. It is about what happens when you are with them. Are you authentic? Are you able to be present, share their stories and be there for them? Do you let them know they matter to you? Do you challenge them when they need it? Do you welcome their feedback to you? Are you the kind of friend to them that you would want a friend to be?

This is where I go to the cosmic nature of relationships. Love has no limits or time. When you love people, appreciate them, see them as valuable to you because of how much they enrich your life, it doesn't matter if you haven't been together in years.

When you reconnect, you just catch up and go from there.

And this only happens if you see yourself as a lifelong learner, eager to grow and share with those around you.

What a blessing!

Don't Try to Do It Alone

Chapter 10:

You Can Give, But Can You Take?

Feeling alone is a common human condition. Add feeling misunderstood and the problem multiplies. I became a helpaholic to gain a sense of belonging, however misguided that notion was! The more I did for people, the more I felt I was a part of things. What it set up was a pattern of me giving and not noticing that I wasn't in fair exchange. This is one of the most difficult things I have had to learn in my life:

Step 10: Learn to actively receive.

That may sound strange, but it is true. Helpaholics are much more skilled at giving than receiving!

And we've all heard the adage: it is better to give than receive. Problem is, when you take something that is true and overdo it, it can really backfire on you!

Since this is my confessional, I'll start with one of my first areas of how this applies to me.

Not realizing help is available.

By being so ready to help others, I could easily start down a path with a sense that I am fully responsible for situations and outcomes and not take advantage of the innumerable people around me who want to contribute, participate, give me help. In that moment, it doesn't occur to me that help is available. I actually end up alienating people because they see me as so in charge, so capable, that there is no room for them. Then they "give up" and expect me to handle things!

Another important aspect of this: when we ask others for help, often they like it! When I call my friend Lida and say I need help with something, her immediate response is: "I'm on the job! What do

> *I want you to take notice that I said "when we ask others for help." This is an important differentiator in the life of a helpaholic.*

you need?" She has told me many times over how great it feels to be needed when someone asks for help! We know we can count on each other. But if I limit my asking for help to her, I don't get to experience the wisdom of others, and they don't get to feel valued when I ask them for help.

What I realized recently is that it comes across as a form of arrogance when I don't reach out to people. It sets me up as some kind of "above it all" person. Which is definitely *not* the case! I get caught up in my own difficulties just like everyone else. But if I don't talk about them, if I don't reach out and ask for advice, feedback or support, people assume I've got it all handled.

Being so focused on doing, I lose track of how to just "be there."

When we're on a mission, that is pretty much all we think about. We're focused, moving toward achieving our goal. I can get like that in my helpaholic phase. So I'm less likely to pick up signals of what is really going on around me. I might not hear what someone is saying, only what I think they are saying.

It takes me out of the present. It keeps me from a natural flow of give and take. When I'm in that state, I might get so focused on someone else's needs, I pay no attention to my own! And I get into a state of "human doing" instead of "human being." It also hampers my ability to be present for someone who just wants to vent about what's going on, not listen to any suggestions about how to fix it. I have found that my unwanted ideas actually become irritating, the same as when others get into "fix-it" mode with me. We both feel more at ease when we listen and are supportive.

Dating and the art of being so nice that I end up trapped.

I'm not saying there is anything wrong with being nice. But the way I learned to be nice was to take care of others. And that certainly applied to men! As I explained in a previous chapter, I grew up in a culture where women's lives revolved around men. Much to the surprise of many people who only know me as a business woman or outspoken activist, when it came to being in a relationship, it was almost as if a button got pushed and I'm thinking about what nice meal I can cook for him or being way too tolerant of what he wanted to watch on TV or rearranging my schedule to fit his.

It pains me to say that those behaviors weren't forced on my part. They were automatic!

And now that I am looking back, with some wisdom of age, I see that it caused me to attract men who responded quite happily to that kind of treatment and then expected it to continue ad-infinitum.

Which meant I would eventually tire of the situation, get frustrated and stop seeing that person. It doesn't take me as long to break the pattern as it used to, but I have to admit that I am not as interested in dating as I was when I was younger. I'm still open to meeting a great guy, just not anxious about it. Hence, I feel really glad to be home watching TV, doing what I want to do!

I have actually put myself at risk by not letting people help me!

When I had ankle replacement surgery in 2004, I let people help me do things I absolutely couldn't do – like drive me to doctor appointments, etc. I had a ramp built so I could scoot around the house on my Roll-A-Bout, and I got a little cocky thinking I could do everything. I decided to empty the dishwasher, and as I leaned into a cabinet with my right leg extended out behind me, I careened down toward the floor. I was able to fall in a way that didn't damage my ankle, but as I sat there, by myself at 8:00 p.m., knowing there was no one nearby to help me, I felt like an idiot. All the what-ifs started racing through my mind — especially the one where I could have destroyed the surgery I had undergone a few days before.

I started asking my son to come at least a few days a week to help cook for me and keep my house in order. It really scared me to realize how close I came to a disaster.

I wish I could say that I have solved this issue completely, but judging from the difficulty I had in writing this piece, I see I still have a way to go in opening up to be more receptive. I'm not interested in becoming overly needy; however, I can clearly see that overdoing my "self-sufficiency" is just as big a detriment to my living the life I would love to live.

Chapter 11:

What Needs to Change?

After struggling through Step 10 and facing that I have had a major difficulty in learning how to receive with grace, it makes perfect sense that the next step is:

Step 11: Learn to do things differently so you only do what you love.

Learning to be open and receptive is first on my list! So, today I have already put a call in to my friend, Judy to ask her for help on a QuickBooks problem.

However, this subject actually goes deeper than asking for help. It requires a re-examination of our mindsets, habits, and "go-to" methods in all aspects of our lives.

But wait, you say! There are so many things I have to do, how can I only do what I love?

The secret is to change your perspective. Let's start with something seemingly minor that has actually been a source of conflict in many households: taking out the trash. It becomes a major issue! So how can you love to take out the trash?

Do you care about having a clean house? Are you irritated because you think someone else should do it? Do you feel it is beneath you? The way I learned to love doing it is by asking myself those questions and more, to the point that I realized my values were actually

> *When I understood that tasks honored my values, I enjoyed them.*

being met when I participated in the things that keep my home the happy, healthy place I want to live. Once I got there, taking out the trash became a pleasant task. In fact, because my alley is really far from the back of my house, I created a sort of Zen practice of loading the two bags (recycling and regular trash) into the back of my car and driving it around. Each time I do it, I feel accomplished.

It can't all be that simple! What about really difficult things I have to do?

Once again, it requires a change in perspective. One of my teachers taught me a process years ago that I find myriad applications for: linking what needs to be done with your higher purpose.

Say you want to be a lawyer, and to work your way through school, you have a part-time job in a warehouse stacking boxes. How can you learn to love doing it?

Ask yourself: What skills are needed to get an education to become a lawyer, and what skills are needed once you've graduated? Discipline, an ability to assess situations and create order out of them, learning to prioritize, the ability to cooperate, willingness to follow a schedule, the ability to complete tasks in a timely manner, healthy respect for authority, an understanding of the whys and hows of getting things done... all can be learned by being great at stacking boxes! And if you are focused on what you are learning and how it is helping you get where you want to go, to fulfill your higher purpose, it is easy to love doing it.

It does require an attitude adjustment. Many times people approach work as a form of drudgery. An odious task that you have to do. But if you see it as a stepping stone to the next phase, find how it can lead you to greater achievements, and link that to what is really important to you – it can actually be fun!

So maybe that can work with physical labor, what about more challenging things, like organizing records and paying taxes? Talk about an odious task!

When I was 17 and my sister was 19, our parents sent us to Europe. We picked up a little Volkswagen Bug in Munich and drove through Austria, Italy, southern France on our way to a school in northern Spain where we would spend five weeks to learn Spanish. This was 1965 and the world was very different... however, Europe was and still is a place to see what effect various governments have on roads, businesses, and the lifestyles of the people who live there. I saw how the roads and countryside were neat and tidy in Austria; then immediately over the border into Italy, everything changed into haphazard, disorganized chaos! I was amazed! Two-lane roads became danger zones, as cars and trucks would drive sometimes four abreast with no regard for safety or order. For a teenager, it was an adventure. My sister didn't know how to drive a stick shift in the beginning, so I started out the trip doing most of the driving. It was fun! But looking back, I understand how easily we could have been in danger.

We stopped at pensions along the way, very inexpensive alternatives to hotels, usually run by families. Through Italy and southern France, we were able to learn a little bit about the local cultures and see how limited most of the people's lives were. They lived and worked in the same way their families had for generations, very few even considering venturing away from their home bases. We were an oddity to them, two young sisters, traveling alone. We had no idea how strange it actually was.

We were so naïve that we parked on a public street in Barcelona, once we finally crossed into Spain, and while we were in a restaurant, the car was broken into and half of our luggage was stolen. We reported it to the police, but they told us we were foolish to leave things in our car and did nothing to help us recover it. Spain was run by a dictator then, Francisco Franco, and there was little accountability to be found.

I'm telling you this long, drawn-out story to show you where I learned to appreciate living in the good old USA. When we returned to the States in late August that summer, I wanted to kiss the soil. And every time I travel out of the U.S., no matter where I've been, I feel like kissing the soil when I get back.

The services we take for granted (postal, police, good roads, well-run cities) and despite all the challenges we face, we are still better off here than any place I have visited.

So when it comes time to pay taxes, I do it with joy. I am so grateful to live here. Even though I'm not happy about the policies of our current government leaders, I'm not so unhappy that I don't feel there is hope of change. The people I met in Spain way back then had no hope of change. It took Franco's death to end the nationalist dictatorship in 1975 and even more time for Spain to become a different kind of country. There is still turmoil there!

So what I'm saying here is that learning to do things differently requires understanding things differently – looking at the big picture and being proactive in how you approach things. Which is vastly different from being reactive and carrying a chip-on-the-shoulder attitude about how difficult you have it.

It requires a change in perception, a change in perspective.

To love paying taxes means you see things differently. It doesn't mean you don't try to get great deductions and lower your tax bill. It means that in the grand scheme of things, you understand that in order to live in a society that actually serves its people, there needs to be some form of government and the people need to pay for it.

So we keep paying for it even when we aren't in favor of some of the policies and laws, and because we are participants, we have the right to work toward changing it.

This big-picture thinking applies not just to how we see our country, it also makes sense in dealing with personal relationships, work situations, any involvement with other people. I've learned to look for the other side to the story. I've learned that no matter how much I want people to do things my way, they have their own ways and are entitled to make their own choices. So when I spend time with people, I make sure that I'm taking care of myself, and if it is no longer compelling to be in certain conversations, I exit. If I don't feel comfortable in a situation, I remove myself as quickly as possible. I pay attention to how I feel and act accordingly. Do I do it to hurt others? No. I do it in as pleasant or unobtrusive way as possible in order to make sure I get to do what I want.

But I try to see things from their point of view at the same time. I've learned that it is okay not to enjoy situations just because someone else does. I've learned to be honest along with being nice, which takes me out of having to make "nice-nice" and brings me into being authentic. I've learned to say no as pleasantly as I can say yes.

And because it all starts with a higher purpose, I can much more easily discern what works for me and what doesn't. My higher purpose is: "I believe we are here to love ourselves, each other and our lives, master the business of life and turn our lead into gold." I can measure tasks, opportunities and all other forms of activities against the standards in my life that come from that higher purpose. If those things aren't part of staying on my self-directed, purposeful path, I can easily decline and feel great about it.

So learning to do things differently really means seeing things differently and acting accordingly?

Yes. That's why I only do what I love to do.

Chapter 12:

The Most Important Thing

I started writing these steps to help myself break patterns that were in the way of my being able to live my life fully, the way I want. I'm not fantasizing that I can sail through the next 20 or so years without challenges or difficulties. I actually welcome those, as they keep me growing.

I just don't want to be the major obstacle in my life!

Creating the first six steps enabled me to look at the habits of thinking that were keeping me stuck, sort of in a revolving door of experiences. The first thing I had to do was allow myself to feel the shame of not having moved beyond them sooner. I credit people like Brené Brown and Oprah Winfrey, and the ever-growing number of women in the #MeToo movement for helping all of us look at our lives more objectively. Realize that we are all vulnerable to our childhood patterns, the social mores we were raised by, the institutionalized standards that we were taught to believe in.

Breaking out of those, freeing ourselves from societal expectations takes courage, and the first thrust usually includes anger at what got us there in the first place. I'm not speaking against anger. I think it fuels our fire, helps us step up and step out. A necessary phase of growth and change.

So I spent some energy venting my anger and frustration at family, educational institutions, political systems, business associates, all those elements that seemed to thwart my ability to feel whole and worthwhile. It is similar to what I learned 25 years ago with a bio-energetics therapist who taught me to raise my fists and beat the bed to release pent up anger and frustration. Very helpful! It cleared the energy so I could think straight.

In the years following that therapeutic experience, I fervently studied with various teachers to help me find answers, find peace in my heart. Each one of those phases of learning led me to understand and develop ways to utilize the next five steps, become more adept at making my life work for me. Those steps continue to lead me back to one basic principle, the one that I use to continue to guide me through whatever uncomfortable, unpleasant or devastating opportunities for growth show up:

Step 12: Live a life of gratitude.

I hear a lot about the concept of gratitude. Most people find it easy to be grateful for the things they really want or like in their lives. But what about the things we don't like?

So here is a shortcut to some of what I've learned to be grateful for:

- **I'm glad my parents didn't coddle or over-nurture me.** They were great at providing food, clothing, and shelter – not so great at helping me or my sisters feel good about ourselves. Since we are all in our late 60s/early 70s, this isn't surprising. Back then, children truly were to be seen and not heard. We learned a lot about life from them; we just had to figure out what it all meant pretty much on our own. Not feeling so connected to my parents or my sisters led me early on to create what has become my family of choice, which is a bigger blessing than I can easily describe. This has freed me up to spend my energy where it really matters to me. I love that!

- **I am deeply grateful that the three men I married and divorced by the time I was 42 taught me that I am much happier and fulfilled living a life that works for me than if I were putting up with behavior and mindsets that are contrary to my inner sense of myself.** I do not wish them ill; however, I have no need to revisit the past with them, think through why it didn't work, etc. I am free to make my own choices. Marriage just isn't my calling in this lifetime. I am thrilled for those who have found a deep connection with someone, whether married or not, and I am great with knowing I may live out my later years on my own. I did work out the whys many years ago, which is probably why I now feel so liberated. I love being my own person!

- **I am also deeply grateful for the difficult men I had to work with for the 29 years of my Miller & Associates life.** I did make some great friends with some of the men in my industry, especially the ones who worked for me. But there were some real doozies out there who 1) didn't think women belonged in the commercial food service equipment industry, 2) were more interested in their egos than doing the right thing, 3) who practiced the art of one-upmanship to perfection, 4) who felt threatened, perhaps, or just really angry that I was able to make a success of our business, and 5) enjoyed thwarting me just for the fun of it.

- **Instead of giving those guys the satisfaction of "winning," we just kept on going and, with the support and drive of some amazing employees and some great factories we represented, created a very successful business that is still going strong 12 years after I sold it to two of my sales guys.** They honored what we had built together by keeping most systems in place, and I am very proud to say they expanded and improved on it exponentially. That experience brings me so much joy!

- **I have a depth of gratitude for the people who have moved on into directions that don't include me.** Instead of feeling discounted or discarded, I've learned that when people self-select out of my life, it is a gesture of authenticity, which I very much appreciate. We are all free to connect with the people and groups we resonate with, enabling us to be far more purposeful and productive.

This is how I turn lead into gold.

I mentioned earlier that I believe we are here to love ourselves, each other and our lives, master the business of life, and turn our lead into gold.

Being grateful is how I do it.

And I have been blessed to work with so many people through the years who have walked that path with me. They have been willing to look at their difficulties, sometimes devastating challenges, and find the blessing hidden in them. It doesn't mean they didn't feel hurt, but it did give them a way to free themselves from living in the pain and moving into the light. If we learn to love the thing we resent, hate, detest, fear, want to get away from, because we see that it has an equal amount of benefit for us, then we are free to move forward and keep learning and growing. When we are stuck in the pain, we are thwarting ourselves, sort of going around in circles, getting nowhere fast.

Margery's Principle

This is how I created my guiding principle in life:

Gratitude, appreciation, and self-discipline are the keys to freedom.

Gratitude: for what is as it is.

Appreciation: which enhances that gratitude and includes all the individuals and elements in the Universe that brought forth that for which I am grateful.

Self-discipline: I pay attention to what goes in my mind and out my mind; in my ears and out my mouth.

When I activate that principle, I find it much easier to pull myself together, to keep growing and changing, and enjoy the journey that is my life.

The Helpaholic 12-Step Program

1. Add a little cynicism to your life. Learn to ask the question: What's in it for me?
2. Stop taking responsibility for other people's experiences.
3. Be kinder to yourself!
4. Set clear boundaries with family members.
5. Remember that help is the happy side of control!
6. Stop thinking, "With me, it will be different!"
7. Learn the art of proactive waiting.
8. Learn to live in the Fertile Void.
9. Find a group and learn from them.
10. Learn to actively receive.
11. Learn to do things differently so you only do what you love.
12. Live a life of gratitude.

Resources:

Websites to visit:
www.greatgirlsnetwork.org
www.peoplebiz.com

Books to read:

Arrien, Angeles. *The Four-Fold Way: Walking the Paths of the Warrior, Teacher, Healer, and Visionary.* HarperOne, 2013.

Buckingham, Marcus, and Donald O. Clifton. *Now Discover Your Strengths.* The Free Press, 2001.

Resources

Acknowledgments

I'm not sure where to even start to say thank you to all the people who have helped make this book possible! First, to my now departed parents who truly did the best they could do. The blessing they are to me is that they were the ideal parents to bring me into the world and give me the ideal lessons and opportunities to learn and grow. I feel the same about my sisters, whom I love dearly and always will.

Add to that family of origin, my grandparents, so clearly influential in my perception of the world. My Russian Jewish paternal ones gave me a value of ethnicity that I carry to this day. My east Texas maternal ones showed me a culture that I have an affinity for, even though I am far removed from it.

I can only name a few of the women who for me are the defining surround of my world: my best friend of 43 years, Lida Keene, who also graciously agreed to illustrate this book; Harriet Reisman-Snyder and Karen Almond, who are here in Dallas and along with Lida are my constant go-to people for feedback and soul nourishment, plus keep me grounded in the here and now; Nell Merlino, as colleague, dear friend, and mentor for the last 13 years, who keeps challenging me to think differently and inspires me to go further. I also want to thank Sandra Zorilla for helping me clarify the last six steps.

Rollie Blackwell Devlin, Andrea Almond, Lea Kaltenbach, Claire Goldman, Beverly Barry, Jane Murray, Dr. Lona Smith, Judy Watson, Toni Portmann, Amy Halman, Andrea Breitling, Carmen Yates, Christiane Hepfer, Elaine Bernstein, Phyllis Bernstein, Kathleen Covens, Marti Royer, Susie Morrissey, Carol Maier, Nadia Machaira, Caroline Lambert, Gail McDonald, Lynne Sipiora, Neely Duncan, Anastasia Franklin, Maddy Kulkarni, Alida Leykauf, Mary Kate Powers, Sameen Wajid, Maxi Hepfer, Susan Ellis, Jodi Conti, Joanie DeBever, Jolina Karen, and Michelle Ayo – all these women have been soul sisters, mothers, daughters, friends, and allies in different ways for me, to varying degrees, and all of them mean the world to me.

I so appreciate Susan Hoff for joining me to get the Great Girls Network started and continuing to be a support and ally of this new continuing form of Movement.

I am thrilled that Pat Romboletti connected me with Ann Deiterich, who has been flexible and extremely helpful in editing the book.

And as always, I am so grateful to my son, Noah Miller, who has taught me the lessons that only motherhood can give. He is still the light of my life.

About the Author

Margery Miller is a Life Entrepreneur who has enjoyed a varied career path and looks forward to new challenges. She takes each new challenge in stride and incorporates what she learns into the next opportunities as they come along.

President and Owner of PeopleBiz Inc., Margery helps people think! She works with people who are ready to get out of the box and lead more productive, purposeful, meaningful lives. Margery is a seasoned business veteran, having owned and managed a manufacturer's rep agency for 29 years before selling it to her employees and putting her focus on PeopleBiz, her coaching and consulting company, which was a side business during her rep years. She helps people understand how to master the business of life. She has been actively involved with nonprofits for many years and was a longtime member of Social Venture Partners Dallas.

She started the Great Girls Network as an alternative to the "good ol' boys network" she believes has "run the world" for too long!

After growing GGN into a membership organization, she has put her focus on its development. Margery believes ardently in the power of human potential and dedicates her life to helping people find their inner voice, find their higher purpose and create meaningful, productive, effective lives. She lives in the Dallas area, where she was born and still feels is home.